DISCOVERING
EMMANUEL

A Path to a Deeper Relationship with Christ

Maureen C. Fleming

Available from:
Marian Helpers Center
Stockbridge, MA 01263

Prayerline: 1-800-804-3823
Orderline: 1-800-462-7426
Websites: ShopMercy.org
marian.org

ISBN: 978-1-59614-533-7

Publication date: October 1, 2020

Imprimi Potest:
Very Rev. Kazimierz Chwalek, MIC
Provincial Superior
The Blessed Virgin Mary, Mother of Mercy Province
August 10, 2020

Nihil Obstat:
Dr. Robert A. Stackpole, STD
Censor Deputatus
August 10, 2020

MARIAN PRESS
STOCKBRIDGE · MA 01263

ACKNOWLEDGEMENTS

For God and for my family
— I am so thankful to and for you;
love you each beyond words.

Table of Contents

INTRODUCTION

Preparing for the Coming of Christ into Our World and into Our Hearts

I love the conversion story of Saul, whose mission had been to persecute Christians until the day he had an encounter with Christ. Then, everything changed. This "change" is what happened to me, as you'll read in the first section of this book. Most of us at one point or another have walked a path that led us away from God. When we turn back toward Him and make a conscious choice to follow Him, conversion begins. It begins in the heart and makes its way to our attitudes, our beliefs, and our actions.

After my testimony, you will find 42 days' worth of daily Scriptures drawn especially from the Advent and Christmas seasons. Alongside the Scriptures, you will find reflections and prayers designed to help you in your own journey to discover Emmanuel, God with us. As you read, I recommend you have a Bible close at hand to refer to the Scriptures I mention throughout. I pray you use this work to reflect upon the significance of the birth of Christ and how the events surrounding His birth continue to be relevant today, in your daily lives. While I hope the content of this book is of value, the greatest value will be in how you use it to connect with and to deepen your intimacy with He who loves you so dearly.

"When you call me, and come and pray to me, I will listen to you. When you look for me, you will find me. Yes, when you seek me with all your heart, I will let you find me — oracle of the LORD — and I will change your lot ..." (Jer 29:12-14).

With peace and blessings,
Maureen

PART ONE
My Story

For I know well the plans I have in mind for you —
oracle of the LORD — plans for your welfare and
not for woe, so as to give you a future of hope. When
you call me, and come and pray to me, I will listen
to you. When you look for me, you will find me. Yes,
when you seek me with all your heart, I will let
you find me — oracle of the LORD — and I will
change your lot; I will gather you together from
all the nations and all the places to which I have
banished you — oracle of the LORD — and bring
you back to the place from which I have exiled you
(Jer 29:11-14).

I was proud to be a Cunningham. My dad was pretty strict with the five of us. While I did not like being on the receiving end of his discipline, I never questioned his love for me. He definitely had a soft side. My mom was always there for me. She carted me around to games and swim meets, volunteered in the Parent-Teacher Organization, and on top of that, while I was sleeping, she went to work. She was a labor and delivery nurse. After her shift ended on Sunday mornings, she went to the hospital chapel for Mass. That left my dad in charge of church duty. Each Saturday evening while my mom was preparing dinner, catching up on chores, or sometimes dying her hair, my dad would load us up and take us to Mass. He pretty much had us under control. We still joke about how it did not matter where we sat in the pew, he could reach over and give us a good, strong squeeze on the knee if we were misbehaving.

My involvement in parish life went a little beyond Mass and CCD classes. On Fridays during Lent, a group of us walked from school to the church for the Stations of the Cross. At Christmas, I was in the pageant. I must confess that some of my favorite church memories are of the annual bazaar and of the summer carnival. I still remember riding the Roundup and eating fried dough. How fun those days were!

Adolescence hit, and I found myself in some trouble. Typical teenage stuff; nonetheless, I needed a fresh start. I transferred from the public school to the Academy of the Holy Family, an all-girl Catholic boarding school. It was a smaller, more structured environment. I needed that.

The Sisters of Charity had a beautiful chapel. Sometimes I would go there to talk to God and tell Him what was on my mind. Other times, I just sat quietly. It was peaceful, and I felt close to Him there. Gradually, within my new surroundings, I was able to make better choices. Shortly after getting back on the right track, my visits to the chapel grew further apart.

Life was moving along. I graduated from high school, then college. I became a teacher, a wife, and then a mother. Throughout that time, I had drifted away from conversations with God. I rarely went to church, yet we did go to the Pre-Cana classes and were married in the Church. After our first son was born, we went to the baptismal prep class so he could be baptized. A few years later, our second child was born. It was right after her birth that my dad died. I was overwhelmed with grief. I remember receiving a mix of greeting cards in the mail — sympathy for the loss of my dad and congratulations on the birth of my new little girl. My emotions ran wild as the pain of loss and the joy of new life were intertwined.

I thought about having our new little one baptized. I figured I should make a few appearances at church, so at least my face would be familiar to the priest. After a few Sundays of attendance, I called the rectory to see about scheduling the Baptism. I was told that we were required to attend another baptismal prep class. I tried to get out of it because we had already attended one class with our first born. No such luck.

The instructor was a gentleman from the parish who explained that the focus of this second class was a bit different from that of the first. He said the first child's Baptism typically was a time when parents were busy with the preparations: selecting the baptismal gown, preparing the guest list, and taking care of details like choosing the party menu. While he did not dismiss the importance of these, he wanted us to reflect more deeply on the meaning of the Sacrament and on our reason for seeking it. He also asked us to think about how we were helping our first born to grow in his Christian faith. Hmmm … .

The instructor shared some of his own journey. He said he had gone through a long period of time where he rarely thought about his faith and only went to church for weddings or funerals. I could relate; I was *still* in that phase. He spoke of his own childhood and his Catholic upbringing, explaining that once he had become a parent, he recognized the importance of his own faith and wanted to lay a similar foundation for his children. His starting point was going to Mass. I thought so much about my dad who had always gone to church. I thought about the foundation he and my mom had laid for me. I left that class motivated and inspired to keep going to Mass even after my daughter's baptismal ceremony. My resolve did not last long.

Life continued, but after the death of my dad, something had changed inside of me. I had all this hurt and did not know what to do with it. I felt angry, lost, and insecure. For the most part, I could put on a mask and act like everything was fine, but by the time I came home from work each day, that mask would wear away. I took my emotions out on my husband and blamed him for my unhappiness. As a result, my marriage became stressed and distant.

One night my mom came over for dinner. Per usual, my husband and I had gotten into a fight. I was frustrated, and hoped to gain a little sympathy from my mom. Her take was that *it was all my fault*, and that I was mean to my husband. As I attempted to defend my character, she said something along these lines: *"You can't hide who you really are from those who know you best."* Ouch! Deep down, though, I knew she was right. I wanted things to get better, and realized I could not keep blaming my husband for our situation. I needed to take a good look at myself and deal with what was happening inside of me.

I found myself *wanting* to go to church. My husband had no interest in joining me and certainly did not understand my new-found desire. There was so much tension on Sunday mornings. It was difficult to get out the door; but once I made it to that pew, it felt good to be in God's house. One Sunday, I saw a bulletin announcement. The parish was seeking volunteers to begin a bereavement ministry. I joined and later our new pastor, Fr. Ray, gifted us each with a New Testament Bible. He referred to it as *The Love Letter*. Though it would be some time before I would read it, I had, on a small scale, begun to reach out to God. I had even made up a little song:

Good morning, Lord.
It's to You that I pray.
Please help me to have a very special day.
Let me bring love and kindness in all that I do.
Let me be a light shining brightly for You.
It's for this, Lord, that I think I am here.
So Lord Jesus Christ, please answer my prayer.

One day, I opened up that *Love Letter* and began to read it. I came upon Matthew 5:14-16: "You are the light of the world. A city set on a mountain cannot be hidden. Nor do they light a lamp and then put it under a bushel basket; it is set on a lampstand, where it gives light to all in the house. *Just so, your light must shine before others*, that they may see your good deeds and glorify your heavenly Father." I reread it and thought about the words to my little song. I wanted to be a good person. I wanted so desperately for my light to shine, but somewhere along the line my light had gone out.

Then, one special Sunday, I sat in church and listened to a visiting pastor tell the story of Jonah. God had told Jonah to go to Nineveh to deliver a message of repentance, mercy, and forgiveness. The Ninevites were Jonah's enemies. I imagine the last thing he wanted to do for them was to serve as an agent of God's mercy. Instead of following God's command, Jonah headed in the opposite direction, away from Nineveh and away from God.

I sat in the pew and was thinking about how God had spoken to Jonah and how Jonah knew what God wanted of him. I felt jealous and even a little angry. I cried out to God, "At least Jonah knew what you wanted of him! Why can't you speak to me the way you spoke to Jonah?"

> I love the LORD, who listened
> to my voice in supplication,
> Who turned an ear to me
> on the day I called (Ps 116:1-2).

What followed seemed at first coincidental. I went to the gas station, and the attendant spoke to me about how beautifully God had created the world. He asked God to bless me. I went to the Chinese restaurant. My fortune cookie read, "*God has given you special blessings.*" While praying a Hail Mary, I noticed these brilliant bluish, purple colors in the sky. Honestly, I had never noticed those colors in the sky before, except in a picture that I had of the Blessed Mother. Something more than coincidence was going on.

I talked to Sr. Jude, my former high school teacher, about the "coincidences" I had been experiencing. She explained to me that God does speak to us — we just don't always hear him. She directed me to a "Life in the Spirit" seminar, where I learned more about God's love. I learned how to enter into and live in relationship with the Lord. I started to spend time in prayer every day and began connecting with Him. The more I sought Him, the more I found Him. A child-like excitement was bubbling up within me. Still, there were times when I questioned the reality of it all. I needed so much confirmation, and that was exactly what I received. One morning while praying I asked, "God, is this really you?" Later, I read Joel 2:27: "I, the LORD, am your God, and there is no other … ."

More and more, I began to recognize God's presence. My sister found a book in her attic and gave it to me. I had not seen it in decades but immediately recognized it: *God is Everywhere* by Barbara Burrow. I opened it and saw the markings on the title page. There was a hand-drawn heart and a penciled-in message saying, "especially in our hearts." As a little girl, I had drawn that heart and written those words. I wondered how I could have forgotten something that had once been so very clear to me: *God is everywhere, especially in our hearts.*

Many years had passed between the day I drew that heart and the day I sat in the pew listening to the sermon about Jonah. When I think back to that day at the church, I am still in awe. When I called out to God, it was as though He was as close to me as my breath. He had always been there. It was I, like Jonah, who had headed in the opposite direction, away from the faith of my childhood and away from God. But when I was ready to turn back, He *did* speak to me. It was not an audible voice that I heard. Even better, He spoke directly to my heart. Through every-day experiences, through the Scriptures, and later in the Eucharist, over and over, He affirmed His great love for me.

> Before I formed you in the womb I knew you ... (Jer 1:5).

> It was not you who chose me, but I who chose you and appointed you to go and bear fruit that will remain, so that whatever you ask the Father in my name he may give you (Jn 15:16).

> Because you are precious in my eyes and honored, and I love you ... (Is 43:4).

As He showered me with His love, my inner being began to change. He brought to me healing, not just from my father's death, but also from life's everyday hurts. The more I came to understand Jesus and the compassion that He had for others, I could not help but to fall in love with Him. I wanted to love the way He did, and I needed Him to teach me His ways. So, I decided to follow Him — best decision ever!

Since then, I have grown in my faith and have come to embrace the religion of my childhood. The Catholic Church has become for me a means to connect with my God, who is so very real. Emmanuel means "God is with us." In the person of Jesus,

He came to show us the way, and He continues to make Himself available to us through His Spirit. No matter where we are on our journey, if we call upon His name, He will meet us. He will walk with us and bless us with the riches of His Kingdom, not just in Heaven, but right here on earth.

> Blessed the one whom you will choose and bring to dwell in your courts. May we be filled with the good things of your house, your holy temple! (Ps 65:5).

PART TWO

Reflections: Into the Loving Presence of the Lord

1. DISCOVER

God is faithful, and by him you were called to fellowship with his Son, Jesus Christ our Lord (1 Cor 1:9).

G od Himself desires for us to live in deep union with Him. He sent His Son to us, in human form, so that we could come to know Him personally, and begin to experience and share His great love for us. Let us ask ourselves, how do we respond to God's desire for us? How do we allow God's presence in our lives to shape who we are? How do we use our unique gifts to bring His love and His light to the world around us?

When my children were young, we used to gather at bedtime during Advent to read and pray together. At the close of our family time, we would light a candle for each child. We would then process together into each child's room as we sang a familiar chant thanking Jesus for giving us His Holy Spirit and telling Him how much we loved Him. Such precious memories I have of us singing our hearts out to the Lord.

Knowing of Jesus and loving Jesus are two different things. My priest, Fr. Ray, would frequently speak of the difference between head knowledge and heart knowledge. We need both to discover and to fully live out our Christian purpose. We have to learn about Christ, His life, and His teachings, but we also have to experience Him and His abiding love for us. Those experiences, living with Him in a relationship every day, affect us and inspire us to become the person who God intends us to be.

God is real. He is among and within us. And whether you are at a place where you know that with all of your heart and respond to Him openly, or you are at a place where you have yet to discover His true presence, this is your time — your time to set apart with and for Him. This is your time to celebrate who He is and discover who you are because of Him.

Let us pray.

Dear God,
Here I am;
help me to discover, more and more,
Your true presence in and around me.
Amen.

2. REFLECT

*Come, let us go up to the LORD's mountain,
to the house of the God of Jacob, that he may
instruct us in his ways, and we may
walk in his paths* (Is 2:3).

In Matthew 8:5-10, we read about a centurion whose servant was suffering. The centurion believed that Jesus, through His Word alone, had the power to heal. The centurion stepped out in faith and approached Jesus. In doing so, he experienced the power and presence of God.

I am reminded of something my sister-in-law used to say to her children: "You can't get to Heaven on my coat tail!" She knew that at some point her boys had to make their own decisions about their beliefs. If they believed, they would have to step out in faith and pursue their own relationship with God. God wants to be our God, but He will not push Himself on us. Instead, through Jesus, He invites us to come to Him. Once we accept that invitation, He showers us with His love, teaches us His ways, and bestows upon us His sanctifying grace.

Today I invite you to think about your faith by reflecting on the following questions. As you read them, discuss your answers with God. Be honest with yourself and with Him about what you believe, your questions, and your struggles.

Do you believe in God?

Do you believe that God is approachable?

Do you believe that God hears your prayers?

Do you believe that Jesus is the Son of God?

Let us pray.

Dear God,
Please help me to sort through
my convictions, my questions and my struggles.
Help me to reflect upon my beliefs
and approach You with confidence.
Amen.

3. CONSIDER

... for the earth shall be filled with
knowledge of the LORD ... (Is 11:9).

In the Gospel of Luke 10:21-24, Jesus praised God for having revealed Himself to the disciples. In the previous verses, Luke 10:1-20, we learn that Jesus had commissioned His disciples and sent them out to the towns where He would go. As they went from town to town, they offered peace and healing and proclaimed the coming of God's Kingdom. The disciples saw God with their very own eyes as He worked through them. They were in awe! Jesus later told them, "Blessed are the eyes that see what you see" (Lk 10:23).

When Adam and Eve were in the Garden of Eden, God talked directly with them. They knew Him intimately. God wanted their lives to be filled with goodness. He told them not to eat of the tree of knowledge of good and evil. He even warned them that doing so would result in death. Adam and Eve chose not to listen to God. As a result, they had to leave Paradise and begin a life that was very different from that which God had planned for them.

God's desires for His children have not changed. He continues to want only goodness for us. He wants us to see Him, to know Him, and to live in union with Him, now and forever. Just as Adam and Eve were given a choice, so, too, are we. If He is to be our God, we have to agree to follow His command. What does He command? The answer is clear in Luke 10:27: "He said in reply, 'You shall love the Lord, your God, with all your heart, with all your being, with all your strength, and with all your mind, and your neighbor as yourself.'" When such is our intent, we will be blessed with eyes that see and ears that hear.

Take some time today to consider God's command. How will you respond?

Let us pray.

Dear God,
Help me to seriously consider Your invitation
To enter into a loving relationship with You.
Help me to begin to understand
what You desire for and from me.
Amen.

4. GO

This is the LORD to whom we looked ...
(Is 25:9).

In Matthew 15:29-37, we read that Jesus went up on the mountain by the Sea of Galilee. There, the crowds followed Him. The sick were brought to Him, and they were healed. After three days, He called together His disciples and expressed concern for the crowds because they had not eaten. He took the fish and the loaves of bread, and He performed a miracle. "They all ate and were satisfied" (Mt 15:37).

At every Mass, Jesus continues to heal and to nourish His followers. By the power of the Holy Spirit, ordinary bread and wine are changed into the Body and Blood of Christ. In John 6:56, Jesus had said to His disciples, "Whoever eats my flesh and drinks my blood remains in me and I in him." Some of His followers neither understood nor accepted this teaching, and they turned away from Him.

Imagine if Mary had turned away when the angel told her that the Holy Spirit would come upon her and that she would give birth to the Son of God. Mary could not have fully understood what was happening, but deep within her, she believed and trusted in God. Think about it — that same Holy Spirit who blessed a virgin womb is the same Holy

Spirit who at every Mass changes ordinary bread and wine into the Body and Blood of Jesus Christ.

Through the Eucharist, Jesus is as present to you as He was to the crowds that day on the mountain. He loves you and wants to nourish you with Himself. You can turn and walk away in disbelief; or you can go to Him, eat, and be satisfied.

Let us pray.

Dear Jesus,
As I go to Mass, with simple faith,
I want to receive You into my being.
I need Your healing, nourishment and strength.
Amen.

5. LISTEN

Trust in the LORD forever! For the LORD is an eternal Rock (Is 26:4).

In Matthew 7:21, 24-27 we read about the wise man building his house on rock rather than on sand. I am thankful to my parents who passed along that same wisdom to me. When my life began to crumble, it did not take long to remember where to turn. The Lord is my rock, my savior, and my king.

As an infant, my parents and godparents brought me to the Church to be baptized. At this Sacrament of Initiation, they presented me to our community. Our community prayed for me and asked God to give me new life in Him. He cleansed me of original sin, marked me as His own, and gave me the gift of the Holy Spirit. It was then that I received grace to believe in God, to hope in Him, and to love Him. It was then that I was given power through His Spirit to begin to grow in holiness.

Then came the time of my Confirmation, a time where my Christian initiation was to be brought to completion. I was anointed by the Bishop to go forth living the message of Christ and spreading His good news of salvation. Through the anointing I received an outpouring of the Holy Spirit and was given grace to go forward in my mission as "disciple and witness to Christ ..." (*Catechism of the Catholic Church*, 1319).

In the Gospel of Matthew 7:21, Jesus makes it clear that we do not enter His Kingdom simply by calling Him Lord. We have to listen to His teachings and act upon them. At the time of my Confirmation, I was not ready to do that. I thought of my Confirmation as an end to religious education classes, rather than the beginning of my journey through life with Christ. So the gift God had given to me at that time remained unopened. I thank God that His gift had no expiration date.

Take some time to think today about your own Confirmation. Think about whether or not you were ready to "assume the role of disciple and witness to Christ ..." (*CCC*, 1319). Did you activate the gift of the Holy Spirit that God had given to you? If not, are you ready to do so now?

Let us pray.

Dear Lord,
Stir up Your Spirit within me.
Help me to listen and move forward
As Your disciple and witness.
Amen.

6. KNOW

I believe I shall see the LORD's goodness
in the land of the living (Ps 27:13).

In Matthew 9:27-31, we see blind men approach Jesus and ask for healing. Because of their faith in Jesus, "their eyes were opened" (Mt 9:30). I love how the actions of Jesus over two thousand years ago continue to be relevant today. As I read this Gospel, I cannot help but think of my own spiritual blindness. For many years I did not see the realm of God; then my eyes were opened to His presence, within and around me.

I remember reading John 15. Jesus was telling His disciples how much He loved them, and that if they kept His commandments they would always remain in His love. He went on to say, "I have told you this so that my joy may be in you and your joy may be complete" (Jn 15:11). I was far from joyful when I first encountered Christ; but as I read His words, I believed that He could trade my sorrow for His joy. Even through some of the worst days, I trusted Him and clung to that promise. As I sit here today and write these words to you, I can honestly say that I know His joy; it is within me.

Through the Holy Spirit we share in God's divinity. As we allow Him to teach and to guide us, we are filled with his nature, with His goodness.

Take some time today to read and pray this prayer. It was St. Paul's prayer for the Ephesians, and it is my prayer for you.

> For this reason I kneel before the Father, from whom every family in heaven and on earth is named, that he may grant you in accord with the riches of his glory to be strengthened with power through his Spirit in the inner self, and that Christ may dwell in your hearts through faith; that you, rooted and grounded in love, may have strength to comprehend with all the holy ones what is the breadth and length and height and depth, and to know the love of Christ that surpasses knowledge, so that you may be filled with all the fullness of God (Eph 3:14-19).

Let us pray.

Dear God,
Thank You for all
that You want to do in and for me.
Help me to see You
and to know Your love.
Amen.

7. RECONCILE

Yes, people of Zion, dwelling in Jerusalem,
you shall no longer weep; He will be most
gracious to you when you cry out; as soon as
he hears he will answer you (Is 30:19).

Jesus did not come to condemn us. Rather, with love and compassion, He came to free us from sin and separation. He came to bring us back to God, the creator of Heaven and earth and the creator of you and me. Through the Sacrament of Reconciliation, the Church continues the ministry of Jesus. The practice includes first examining your conscience then confessing your sins before the priest. As we engage in this Sacrament, showing sorrow for our offenses to God and to others, the priest, who acts in the person of Jesus, grants us absolution. Matthew 18:18 — "Amen, I say to you, whatever you bind on earth shall be bound in heaven, and whatever you loose on earth shall be loosed in heaven."

Jesus knew the strength of sin and the weaknesses of humans. He knew we would need healing and restoration. As we seek Him in this Sacrament, we not only receive forgiveness but also grace — grace to strengthen our resolve to abandon sin and follow Him.

My daughter helped to facilitate a retreat for second graders who were receiving the Sacrament of Reconciliation for the first time. She carried a heavy backpack to show the children how sin can weigh you down. She then simulated a confession and showed the young children how participating in the Sacrament and receiving God's forgiveness and grace is just like removing a heavy backpack from your shoulders.

Today, consider lightening your load. Read Exodus 20:1-17. This Scripture passage will help you to thoroughly examine your conscience. Then, go, receive the Sacrament. If you have not been in some time and have forgotten the procedure, just tell the priest it has been a while since your last Confession. He is acting in the person of Christ; with love and understanding, he will guide you through. As you are absolved of your sins, you will leave free to move forward in His perfect light.

Let us pray.

Father God,
Search my being.
Help prepare my heart and soul
For a thorough, honest confession.
Amen.

8. GIVE

Like a shepherd he feeds his flock;
in his arms he gathers the lambs ...
(Is 40:11).

In the Gospel of John, Jesus says, "Amen, amen, I say to you, unless you eat the flesh of the Son of Man and drink his blood, you do not have life within you. Whoever eats my flesh and drinks my blood has eternal life, and I will raise him on the last day" (Jn 6:53-54).

I was invited to attend a dedication ceremony at a non-denominational church. At the end of the service, there was an altar call where anyone who wanted to give their heart to Jesus was invited to come forward. It was beautiful. I remember asking God why we did not have an altar call at our Catholic Church. I kid you not, a short time later I was sitting in the pew at Saint Mary's listening to a visiting priest. During his talk, he paused and said, "And for those of you who ever wondered why we don't have an altar call ... we do. It is called the Eucharist." He continued, "Every time you come to the altar, the Eucharistic Minister lifts up the Eucharist and says 'the Body of Christ.' We reply 'Amen.' Our Amen means I believe and I receive." I remember that frequently, now, as I go to the altar to receive Jesus in Holy Communion. I say "Amen" aloud and then oftentimes, in an inner whisper, tell Him that I believe and I receive Him. I know He hears me, and I know I am as close to Him as I can possibly be while still here on this earth. In the Eucharist, we more than receive Him into our hearts; we receive Him in all fullness — Body, Blood, Soul, and Divinity. As His Body and Blood mixes with ours, we are intertwined. We become one. "For my flesh is true food, and my blood is true drink. Whoever eats my flesh and drinks my blood remains in me and I in him" (Jn 6:55-56). The *Catechism of the Catholic Church* teaches, "That in this sacrament are the true Body of Christ and his true Blood is something that 'cannot be apprehended by the senses,' says St. Thomas, 'but only by faith, which relies on divine authority.' For this reason, in a commentary on Luke 22:19 ("This is my body which is given for you.'), St. Cyril says: 'Do not doubt whether this is true, but rather receive the words of the Savior in faith, for since he is the truth, he cannot lie'" (*CCC*, 1381; St. Thomas Aquinas, *STh* III,75, 1; cf. Paul VI, *MF* 18; St. Cyril of Alexandria, *In Luc.* 22, 19: PG 72, 912; cf. Paul VI, *MF* 18.).

Many of Jesus' disciples struggled with this teaching and turned away. John 6:67-69: "Jesus then said to the Twelve, 'Do you also want to leave?' Simon Peter answered him, 'Master, to whom shall we go? You have the words of eternal life. We have come to believe and are convinced that you are the Holy One of God.'"

Let us pray.

Dear Lord,
Thank You for completely giving
Yourself to me.
Help me to learn how to give myself
completely to You.
Amen.

9. BECOME

*Then astonishment seized them all and they
glorified God, and, struck with awe, they said,
"We have seen incredible things today"*
(Lk 5:26).

Faith is a gift from God, which we who have been
baptized already have within our being. It can lie
dormant, or it can grow. Growth begins with action
on our part.

In Luke 5:19-20, 24-25, we see a clear example
of faith-filled action: "But not finding a way to bring
him in because of the crowd, they went up on the
roof and lowered him on the stretcher through the
tiles — into the middle in front of Jesus. When he
saw their faith, he said, 'As for you, your sins are
forgiven.' ... . 'But that you may know that the Son
of Man has authority on earth to forgive sins' — he
said to the man who was paralyzed, 'I say to you,
rise, pick up your stretcher, and go home.' He stood
up immediately before them, picked up what he had
been lying on, and went home, glorifying God."

This man reached out to Jesus. Jesus forgave
his sins and proved His authority to do so through a
powerful healing. Can you imagine witnessing such
power? Can you imagine experiencing such love and
mercy? How this man's faith must have been solid-
ified! On the other hand, the Pharisees were also

among the crowd. They questioned His authority, rejected His claim to be the Son of Man, and even participated in His Crucifixion.

Over and over again in the Scriptures we see examples of those who rejected Christ and of those who chose to follow. Christ's faithful, those who believed and accepted Him, went on to experience God's plan of Salvation. They, through Christ's life, death, and Resurrection, were set free from the rule of sin. The separation between them and the Almighty One was no more!!!

Let us pray.

Dear Jesus,
Please fill me with faith
that I may become and remain
one of Your followers.
Amen.

10. GRASP

And if he finds it, amen, I say to you, he rejoices more over it than over the ninety-nine that did not stray (Mt 18:13).

Throughout Scripture, we see how God wants to relate to us and how He wants for us to relate to Him. As we imitate the interactions we see in the Scriptures, we come to know Him personally. We begin to understand the deep love He has for us and the reality that only with Him are we complete.

One of my middle school students came to me one day, and told me that he had lost a piece of his watch. That whole day, he searched for it. Finally, as the school day was about to come to a close, he came running to me. With great excitement, he yelled, "I found the missing piece!"

That day on my way home, I stopped at the Adoration Chapel around the corner from my school and spent some time in prayer. In the stillness, I felt a sweet familiarity. It was a connection with my Creator. It occurred to me that I, too, had found the missing "peace" — His name was Jesus.

The next morning was the anniversary of my father's death. My mom was having a Mass said for him. I arrived at the church where I had been raised, and was thinking about the previous day's events. I heard the hymn, "Hosea" by Gregory Norbet. Hearing this song was not a coincidence. I felt like I had been the lost sheep that we read about in Matthew 18:12-14. Jesus had indeed found me. I know He was rejoicing.

Let us pray.

Dear God,
Help me to grasp the extent
to which You yearn for me.
Amen.

11. TURN

Merciful and gracious is the LORD, slow to anger,
abounding in mercy (Ps 103:8).

As we spend time with God, reading the Scriptures and talking with Him, not only do we come to know Him personally, but we also come to know ourselves. Some of what we find is not always so good.

God, however, is all good. In Psalm 103:8, God is described as "merciful, gracious, slow to anger, abounding in mercy." These traits are seen throughout the Scriptures. Remember the story of the adulteress (John 8:2-11). The Scribes and Pharisees brought this sinful woman to Jesus and asked what He would say. They knew that according to the law, she was to be stoned to death. Jesus challenged the crowd to look within themselves. He said that whoever among them was without sin could go ahead and cast the first stone. Not one could do so. As the crowd went away, Jesus turned to her. With love and compassion, He set her free and told her to turn away from sin.

The Father created us to be wonderful, holy people. Along with our human nature, He gave us free will. Our human nature, disordered by original sin passed down to us from Adam and Eve, predisposes us to sin. Sin separates us from God and inhibits us from becoming that which we were created to be. Thank God, though, because He did not just leave it at that. He devised a plan to bring all of creation back to Himself. The plan: Salvation through His Son, Jesus Christ. Salvation begins right here on this earth and continues throughout eternity.

Today, take a look within yourself. In what areas could you use a little of the Lord's pardoning, mercy and grace?

Let us pray.

Dear Jesus,
Help me to turn away from sin
and turn toward You.
Amen.

12. BLESS

I will extol you, my God and king; I will bless your name forever and ever (Ps 145:1).

I regularly pray the Rosary. This devotion helps me to stay close to God and helps me to try to live a better life — one that is a little less selfish, a little more loving, and a little more compassionate. When I think about the Annunciation and the Visitation, I am so inspired by Mary's actions. She truly is my greatest model of discipleship. First, at the Annunciation, the angel came to Mary and told her that she would conceive the Son of God himself. Here we see her example of simple trust and complete surrender. In the Visitation, Mary carries on in her service to God, traveling to visit her cousin Elizabeth who, though beyond the child bearing years, had also conceived a son. Let's read the exchange that took place between these two women:

> When Elizabeth heard Mary's greeting, the infant leaped in her womb, and Elizabeth, filled with the holy Spirit, cried out in a loud voice and said, "Most blessed are you among women, and blessed is the fruit of your womb. And how does this happen to me, that the mother of my Lord should come to me? For at the moment the sound of your greeting reached my ears, the infant

in my womb leaped for joy. Blessed are you
who believed that what was spoken to you
by the Lord would be fulfilled."

And Mary said:

My soul proclaims the greatness of the Lord;
my spirit rejoices in God my savior. For he has
looked upon his handmaid's lowliness; behold,
from now on will all ages call me blessed. The
Mighty One has done great things for me, and
holy is his name. His mercy is from age to age
to those who fear him (Lk 1:41-50).

Mary went to Elizabeth. She shared what was
going on in her own life, and she also supported Elizabeth in her walk. As they came together, they lifted
one another up and gave glory to God. How blessed
they were to have God and to have each other.

Do you have or could you use such a relationship
as this? Today, talk with God about your supports.
Who is your greatest model of discipleship? Who in
your life do you walk with on your faith journey?

Let us pray.

Dear Lord,
With my lips and my actions,
may I bless You,
and may that blessing extend outward.
Amen.

13. EXPRESS

I am the LORD, your God, teaching you how to prevail, leading you on the way you should go
(Is 48:17).

Teach me and lead me, O Lord. When I look back over the years, I can see my growth as a disciple, and in general, as a person. God has shown me how to be more patient with myself and with others, and how to live less selfishly and more for others. This life with His guidance has led me, and continues to lead me, to experience more and more joy, peace, and security.

I remember going to a mission at a neighboring Catholic church. The missionary talked about what it meant to be "saved." Up until that point, I must confess that I thought the word "saved" was only applicable in non-Catholic denominations. The priest at that mission cleared up my misconception.

He addressed the audience as a whole. He asked if we knew that we were sinners. He asked if we were truly sorry for our sins and for having offended God. He asked if we believed that Jesus died on the cross to save us from our sins. He asked us if we wanted to turn from our sins and follow Christ. He said if we said 'yes" to those questions, then we were indeed saved.

I remember thinking, that's all? Well, then, I guess I am saved. Being saved is not an end; being saved is the beginning of a new, extraordinary life. It is a life where God's Spirit leads us and guides us continually. Salvation is a choice, and it is ongoing.

Today consider your understanding of salvation. Have you turned to Jesus, expressed true sorrow for your sins and asked Him to be the Lord of your life? Have you asked Him to fill you with His Spirit?

Let us pray.

Lord Jesus,
I want to follow You.
I want You to be Lord of my life.
Fill me with Your Spirit.
Amen.

14. RISE

*Then we will not withdraw from you; revive us,
and we will call on your name* (Ps 80:19).

In Matthew 17:9, Jesus told His disciples not to
tell anyone what they had seen until after He had
been resurrected. Let us go back into the Scriptures
and try to envision what they had experienced on
the mountain top with Jesus:

> And he was transfigured before them; his
> face shone like the sun and his clothes be-
> came white as light. And behold, Moses
> and Elijah appeared to them, conversing
> with him. Then Peter said to Jesus in re-
> ply, "Lord, it is good that we are here. If
> you wish, I will make three tents here, one
> for you, one for Moses, and one for Eli-
> jah." While he was still speaking, behold,
> a bright cloud cast a shadow over them,
> then from the cloud came a voice that said,
> "This is my beloved Son, with whom I am
> well pleased; listen to him." When the
> disciples heard this, they fell prostrate and
> were very much afraid (Mt 17:2-6).

The disciples had just witnessed Jesus change
from an earthly body into a heavenly body right

before their eyes. And if that wasn't enough, they witnessed Jesus talking to Moses and Elijah. And if that still wasn't enough, they heard the voice of God directing them to listen to Jesus. The Scriptures say the disciples fell on their faces and were afraid. Then, as we read in Matthew 17:7, "But Jesus came and touched them, saying, 'Rise, and do not be afraid.'"

How often do we find ourselves in a situation where we feel some type of fear? How often could we use a gentle touch from Jesus? How often do we need a little help in order to rise?

This is a Scripture that should be kept close to our hearts. First, we all experience some type of fear. When we do, we need to remember that Jesus tells us not to be afraid. Fear may come into our human emotions, but in the depths of the human spirit there is no place for it. Second, Jesus knows what we can do in and through Him. He didn't send those disciples back down the mountain alone. He went with them. He was with them always, as He is with us — giving us everything we need to rise.

Let us pray.

Dear God,
Help me to know without a doubt
that You are always with me,
encouraging me, with Your touch, to rise.
Amen.

15. PREPARE

*The next day he saw Jesus coming toward him
and said, 'Behold, the Lamb of God, who takes
away the sin of the world'* (John 1:29).

When I was a child, I went to Church because
my parents did. As an adult, I go to Church
because I love the Lord. I want to go to His house
to be with Him, to thank Him, and to worship Him.
I want to encounter Him — to be one with Him
— in the most intimate way possible as He offers
Himself to me in the Eucharist.

How do we prepare for such an encounter? We
participate as fully as possible in the prayers and the
rituals, going beyond just the motions. Today let us
focus on the Introductory Rites and the Liturgy of
the Word and how through these parts of the Mass,
we can enter into some God pleasing worship.

When we enter His house and look to the tabernacle, genuflect, and with Holy Water on our finger-
tips, make the Sign of the Cross — we are saying, "In
the name of the Father, and of the Son, and of the
Holy Spirit — I come to worship You, Lord." As the
Mass begins we are surrounded by our brothers and
sisters in Christ. We must listen and fully participate in
these rites. As we do, we become aware of the presence of the Blessed Mother, all the angels, and all the
saints. We are immersed in God's mercy as together

we offer to Him praise, blessing, adoration, and thanks-giving. We acknowledge, as did John the Baptist, that Christ is the "Lamb of God" who takes away our sins. We are ready to move into the Liturgy of the Word where we listen with intent to the word of God. With our minds and our hearts open, we ask the Holy Spirit to enlighten us through the Gospel and the Priest's homily. We must hold that which we have heard ever so close to our hearts.

Let us pray.

Father God,
Teach me, through practice and persistence,
to prepare to encounter You in the Holy Mass.
Amen.

16. PRAY

Remember your compassion and your mercy,
O LORD, for they are ages old (Ps 25:6).

Jesus appeared to St. Faustina on February 22, 1931. She describes the encounter in her diary.

> In the evening, when I was in my cell, I saw the Lord Jesus clothed in a white garment. One hand [was] raised in the gesture of blessing, the other was touching the garment at the breast. From beneath the garment, slightly drawn aside at the breast, there were emanating two large rays, one red, the other pale. In silence I kept my gaze fixed on the Lord; my soul was struck with awe, but also with great joy. After a while, Jesus said to me, "Paint an image according to the pattern you see, with the signature: Jesus, I trust in You" (*Diary of Saint Maria Faustina Kowalska*, 47).

I learned of St. Faustina one day at Mass, as my priest spoke of her humble life in the convent and of her extraordinary relationship with Jesus. He spoke of the Chaplet of Divine Mercy, and encouraged us to pray the Chaplet for the salvation of souls. I quickly embraced St. Faustina and this devotion, because of its simplicity, and because it reminded me of something my grandmother had said to me when I was a little girl. Just after my grandfather had died, she told me it was my responsibility to pray for the soul of my grandfather and for all Holy Souls in Purgatory. The Chaplet seemed to be a simple way to respond to that call.

Take some time to read the words Jesus spoke to St. Faustina; then take some time to pray the Chaplet of Divine Mercy. Know there are many graces drawn from this devotion, for you and for all souls.

Jesus said to St. Faustina:

> ...Tell [all people], My daughter, that I am Love and Mercy itself. When a soul approaches Me with trust, I fill it with such an abundance of graces that it cannot contain them within itself, but radiates them to other souls (*Diary*, 1074).

Let us pray.

Oh Lord,
Fill my soul,
that it may radiate Your grace.
Amen.

17. HONOR

What is your opinion? A man had two sons.
He came to the first and said, "Son, go out and
work in the vineyard today" (Mt 21:28).

In Matthew 21:28-32, we read the parable of the two sons. We see the intent and the actions of both sons. One serves his father in word, not deed. The other serves his father in deed, not word. Today, let us reflect upon the complete, honoring service of Mary and Joseph, who in both word and deed were completely faithful to God and to the Jewish Law.

We are all familiar with the story of Mary and Joseph. They were betrothed when the angel Gabriel came to Mary and announced Mary's role in God's plan of Salvation. Mary honored the will of the Father with her "yes". Joseph learned that Mary was with child and knew that according to the law, Mary would be stoned for committing adultery. He planned to send her away quietly until, of course, the angel gave him different instructions. Joseph honored the will of the Father with his "yes."

God has plans for us too, plans that require our "yes." These plans are not just for our own welfare, but for the welfare of others. Sometimes, we may be uncertain of what is being asked of us. Sometimes, we know but might be a little fearful or uncertain of our own abilities. Read this interaction between God and Moses, and remember that God will always give us everything we need to do His work.

> "Now, go! I am sending you to Pharaoh to bring my people, the Israelites, out of Egypt." But Moses said to God, "Who am I that I should go to Pharaoh and bring the Israelites out of Egypt?" God answered: "I will be with you ..." (Ex 3:10-12).

Let us pray.

Dear God,
Help me to serve You, to honor You,
and to glorify Your Holy Name.
Amen.

18. RECEIVE

Turn to me and be safe,
all you ends of the earth,
for I am God; there is no other!
(Is 45:22).

While I was still grieving the death of my father, I started to go to Mass. I remember how good it felt to just be there, in God's house. I didn't realize it at the time, but what I was experiencing was the peace of Christ.

> Peace I leave with you; my peace I give to you. Not as the world gives do I give it to you. Do not let your hearts be troubled or afraid (Jn 14:27).

Around that time, I went to see my former high school teacher, Sr. Mary Jude. She gave witness to her own need for a Sacramental life. She told me by no mistake was I Catholic. Those words have remained with me, and to that I say, "Amen." Today, I cannot imagine living my life without participating in the Holy Sacrifice of the Mass. I need to gather on the Lord's Day to pray with my brothers and sisters in Christ. I need to take time to call to mind my sins, give thanksgiving and praise to my Creator, and listen to His Word. And ultimately, I need to receive Christ in the Eucharist. In this most intimate of unions, as the Lord draws me to Himself, I am overwhelmed by His desire to be one with me. Fully aware of His loving presence living in me, I am transformed.

After receiving Him and spending a few moments expressing my love and gratitude, I welcome the final blessing from the priest. Filled with the peace of Christ, I am ready to go out and share Him with the whole world.

Let us pray.

Father God,
Thank You for the gift of the Mass.
Thank You for instituting the Eucharist.
Through it, may the whole world receive Your peace and be transformed.
Amen.

19. MEET

Behold, I am sending my messenger ahead of you,
he will prepare your way before you (Lk 7:27).

John the Baptist came with the message to prepare the way for Christ's coming. Some did not heed his message. Upon Christ's coming, some still chose to reject God. Several thousand years later, the same remains. God is still getting overlooked in our world and even in our Church. Some are just not aware of His true presence, which is everywhere in all things, especially in the Holy Mass.

I have heard people say, "I don't get anything out of the Mass." I have seen people turn away from the Catholic Church and the Mass. But, as we encounter the Lord and begin to really understand the structure of Mass and the purpose for our rituals, the Mass becomes an essential, sacred time that we set aside to meet with Him; it becomes a time to come before Him, listen to His Word, worship Him, and be filled with His Body, Blood, Soul and Divinity.

When we go to Mass and ask the Lord to help us to take what we hear, process it in our minds, and embrace it in our hearts, our lives become enriched. When our knowledge moves from our head into our hearts, we are brought into deeper conversion. That conversion is ongoing and simply results in a more beautiful, peaceful life.

When you go to Mass this weekend, arrive early. Tell the Lord that you are there to meet with Him and that your desire is to follow Him. Ask that you may hear His Word and be completely filled with His presence. And as you receive Him in Holy Communion, take time to tell Him that you love Him and that you want to give yourself to Him, in that moment and always.

Let us pray.

Dear God,
Thank You for creating our sacred
meeting place.
Amen.

20. UNDERSTAND

So shall your way be known upon the earth
(Ps 67:3).

I remember a gentleman once told me he thinks the Catholic faith is oppressive. My discovery of the Lord and experience with the traditions and guidance of our Catholic faith has led me to know it is quite the opposite. When we use God's gift of free will to seek and understand His teachings, and then practice those teachings, we find His saving power to be indescribably liberating.

When I told my youngest son that he had to go to swim lessons, he put up quite a fuss. He insisted that he was a "good enough" swimmer. He even boldly questioned me as to why I had not consulted him prior to making such plans for him. I began to explain the benefits of being a strong swimmer, but it became clear that he was not ready to try to understand. I ended the conversation with, "You know Mommy makes decisions based on what is good for you; just trust me on this."

He came to terms with the fact that his participation in the lessons was non-negotiable. Later that evening, we were reading a story about a little girl who was preparing for Holy Communion. The little girl, through her conversations with Jesus, was learning that God would never ask her to do something that was not ultimately in her best interest. My son stopped me and looked at me as if a light bulb had been turned on. His comment indicated his realization that the conversation in the book between God and the little girl mirrored our earlier conversation. I told him things like that were what Fr. Ray would call a "God-incidence." God knows we will not always completely understand His ways, but He does ask us to trust him. The more we trust and step out in faith, the more we experience His wisdom. His wisdom leads us to freedom.

Let us pray.

Dear Lord,
Help me to trust in Your ways.
Amen.

21. ADORE

Behold, the virgin shall be with child and bear a son, and they shall name him Emmanuel, which means God is with us (Mt 1:23).

I remember my first Holy Week after experiencing a conversion of heart. I had this strong desire to go to Mass every day during that week. That, in itself, was amazing. Holy Thursday came and something happened that I had never experienced. At the end of the Mass, there was a procession. The priest was holding something up, and everyone was following. He stopped, and the entire assembly gathered around him. I was at the end of the procession and could not see well. I was curious as to what he was holding.

Sometimes, when I look back, I feel foolish by the limited knowledge I had of my faith. Many times I still feel that way, because there is just so much that I do not know. Then I am consoled as I think of how much the Lord has shown me, and how He continues to delight my heart with new understandings.

I later learned not what the priest was carrying — but Whom. The priest was lifting up the Monstrance, carrying Jesus in the Blessed Sacrament. In the *Catechism of the Catholic Church*, it is explained that "As faith in the Real Presence of Christ in his Eucharist deepened, the Church became conscious of the meaning of silent adoration of the Lord present under the Eucharistic species" (*CCC*, 1379).

God is with us always and everywhere, but nowhere as completely and intimately as in the Eucharist. My parish has a Perpetual Eucharistic Adoration Chapel. Twenty-four hours a day, seven days a week, Christ is present. At least one person is with Him at all times, adoring His Precious Body. Going to that Chapel and sitting in silent prayer has helped me to experience His True Presence.

Find an Adoration Chapel near you or just go and sit before the tabernacle. Pour out your heart to Him and let Him fill you with His loving, peaceful presence.

Let us pray.

Lord,
Help me to set aside time for You —
time to adore You in Your Church,
where Your Presence is Real and True.
Amen.

22. LEARN

Therefore the Lord himself will give you a sign;
the young woman, pregnant and about to bear a
son, shall name him Emmanuel (Is 7:14).

E mmanuel means God is with us. He wants us to
know Him, to learn His ways, and to become
like Him in love and in holiness. John 6:45 says, "It
is written in the prophets: 'They shall all be taught
by God.' Everyone who listens to my Father and
learns from Him comes to me." It is through the
Scriptures that we learn from the Father.

God speaks to us through the Scriptures. The
more we read and learn, the more we are able to
connect the message of the Gospel to our own lives.
The more connections we make, the more we are
able to live out that message.

I have frequently heard the Bible referred to as
"Basic Instructions Before Leaving Earth."

The Church in her wisdom created a cycle of
readings so we would be more familiar with the Scriptures. The readings are compiled in the Lectionary
and are read daily at Mass and on Sundays. Rather
than being organized by the books of the Bible, these
readings follow a sequence from the beginning of the
liturgical year to the end.

There are three cycles of Sunday readings (Years A, B, and C) and two cycles of daily readings (Cycles I and II). There are many Catholic Apps with these readings. They can also be found at http://www.usccb.org/bible/readings. If you do not already have a Catholic website or Catholic app that you use for the daily readings, take some time today to explore. You will find that it only takes a few minutes to check in with God through the daily readings. The time spent is more than worthwhile.

Let us pray.

Father God,
May I continue to learn from You
and follow Your ways.
Amen.

23. FOLLOW

Do not be afraid, Zechariah, because your
prayer has been heard (Lk 1:13).

Zechariah was devout and prayerful (Lk 1:1-25). When God's will was revealed to him, he responded with disbelief. Mary was devout and prayerful. When God's will was revealed to her, she responded with trust. I cannot help but think of my own mother as I think about response to God's will.

My mother had attended a retreat with me. At the end, the women were invited to share. My mother told the group that she had no burdens or problems; she was just happy to be there with her daughter. I later asked her how she could say that she had no burdens or problems, as I have watched her experience sickness, pain, loss, and sorrow. She told me that she is just grateful for all that she has and doesn't like to look at the things that are problematic, as there is nothing she can do about it. I called her again later, because I still wasn't quite satisfied with her answer. It was then that she shared with me something I had not known. Every night she prays one Hail Mary, one Our Father, and an Act of Contrition. Then she prays these words:

> Let me be okay with whatever You have in mind for me: "Be it done to me according to Your will."

Help me not to be afraid.
Take care of my children.
Give them what they need.
Bring them back to You.

Let us pray.

Dear Jesus,
Help me to be devout and prayerful
and to respond to You with trust.
Amen.

24. DEVOTE

Do not be afraid, Mary, for you have
found favor with God (Lk 1:30).

Psalm 24:1-6 touches my heart. It makes me think
of how blessed I am to have a God who loves
me so much that though divine, He invites me to
Himself. The Psalmist proclaims God as the Creator
of the world. Everything in it belongs to Him! The
proclamation is followed by a question: Who has the
right to go to the Lord and stand in His Holy presence? The question is followed by an answer: Those
who seek Him and His holy ways.

God wants us to seek Him and to come to
know Him. God is all about love — our lives are a
love story — between us and God and us and others.
He does not want us to focus on the temporal, on
what is unimportant and fleeting but on Him, whose
love is everlasting.

Today's Psalm not only describes those who
can come before the Lord, but it also includes a
promise to those who do. The promise is that they
will receive blessings.

Devote yourself to Him. Read His Word. Talk
with Him and walk with Him. Then, just as Mary
found favor with the Lord, so will you.

Blessed the one whom you will choose and
bring to dwell in your courts.

May we be filled with the good things of
your house, your holy temple! (Ps 65:5).

Let us pray.

Dear Lord,
Please show me how
to devote more and more of myself
to You.
Amen.

25. REJOICE

The LORD, your God, is in your midst,
a mighty savior,
Who will rejoice over you with gladness,
and renew you in his love,
Who will sing joyfully because of you
(Zeph 3:17).

Just as He longs for us, we too have a longing that can only be satisfied by the Lord, Our God. He desires to draw us near, embrace us with His everlasting love, and fill us with His indescribable joy.

> As the Father loves me, so I also love you. Remain in my love. If you keep my commandments, you will remain in my love, just as I have kept my Father's commandments and remain in his love. I have told you this so that my joy may be in you and your joy may be complete (Jn 15:9-11).

Reflect on the words "joy," "rejoice," and "happiness." They are found over and over again in God's word, revealing to us how much He wants for His joy to be in us. In Luke 1:39-45, Mary greeted Elizabeth and immediately the child within Elizabeth's womb leapt for joy. Merely being in the presence of the Lord created such excitement, such happiness. That is how God wants us all to feel as we come into His presence.

Mary was the first human tabernacle, the first among us to actually have the physical Christ within her. We are blessed to be able to follow in her footsteps. When we go to Mass and receive the Holy Eucharist, we too become a tabernacle, for we receive into our human bodies the Body, Blood, Soul and Divinity of Jesus Christ.

Through Mary, Christ came into the world.
Through you, Christ remains in the world.

Let us pray.

Dear Lord,
I shall rejoice in You
as You come to dwell within me.
Amen.

26. RESPOND

And Mary said:
"My soul proclaims the greatness of the Lord;
my spirit rejoices in God my savior"
(Lk 1:46-47).

In the Old Testament reading of 1 Samuel 1:24-28, we learn of Hannah and her devotion to God. Hannah was barren and desperately wanted to have a child. She went to Eli, the priest, and asked for a special blessing. She made a promise to God that if she were to conceive, she would offer up the child to the service of the Lord. God granted her request, and Hannah kept her promise. When Samuel was about the age of three, Hannah brought him to live with Eli.

I remember when my son began to struggle in his faith journey. I prayed for the Lord to put people in his path — good role models who would help him with his walk. It was then that a new coach took over the school baseball team. My son became friendly with him. As their relationship deepened, I learned that the coach was a Christian. He not only shared his love of baseball with my son, but also shared his love for the Lord.

What does this have to do with Samuel? When Samuel was dedicated to the Lord, he went to live with Eli. One night, Samuel heard a voice calling to him. Thinking it was Eli's voice, Samuel went to Eli. Eli, not having called for him, sent Samuel back to bed. This went on until finally Eli realized that the voice was God's. Eli told Samuel to go back to bed and that the next time he heard the voice calling, he was to respond, "Speak, LORD, for your servant is listening" (1 Sam 3:9). I thank God that my son's coach was listening as God called him into my son's life.

Let us pray.

Dear God,
Help me to respond to Your call
to bring Your love and goodness to others.
Amen.

27. TRUST

Make known to me your ways, LORD;
teach me your paths (Ps 25:4).

In Luke 1:57-66 we read about Elizabeth, wife of Zechariah. She was a strong, faithful woman who, much to the dismay of the crowd, has chosen to name her son John. She didn't give into the crowd. I love how they turn to Zechariah, who in turn confirms Elizabeth's discernment. This is the man who was silenced for his disbelief, when the angel Gabriel announced to him that his wife was to conceive the child who would have a great role in God's plan for salvation. Let us put ourselves in Zechariah's shoes. What must he have been thinking and feeling as he watched the angel's message come to be, as he watched the child grow within the womb of his once barren wife? God definitely had a plan and proved Himself to be faithful.

The word "fear" is used in Luke 1:65. When I think about this word, I think about two definitions: terror, but also amazement. Terror can block amazement, and skepticism can block trust. When we move forward in trust, we are able to enjoy watching the Lord do His mighty works.

Knowing that the Lord's hand is in all things, and trusting Him to move in His way and in His time is a gift — one that develops over time. I pray that the Lord will lead us all more and more to a place of complete trust, a place where we can follow and serve His purpose without trepidation.

Let us pray.

Dear Lord,
Lead me into a deeper trust
that I may see You in all things
and live in awe of Your ways.
Amen.

28. SURRENDER

For today in the city of David
a savior has been born for you who is
Messiah and Lord (Lk 2:11).

It does my heart well to think about our biblical ancestors. Through their stories, their lives, and their interactions with God, I see how He blesses those who seek Him. Through them, my faith is strengthened. I can dwell secure in knowing that as He was with them, so too, He is with me.

In Luke 2:1-14, we read about the birth of Jesus. We all know the story. There was no room for Mary at the inn, so she had to give birth to Jesus in the stable, a place where the animals lay. I do not imagine that Mary's surroundings were an issue for her, as she knew she was blessed by God Almighty. Imagine her joy as she first held baby Jesus in her arms. Then, imagine her emotions as she was visited by the shepherds who spoke of what they saw and heard. Mary and Joseph each had already been visited by an angel, and herein comes a message about a multitude of angels proclaiming the birth of the Messiah.

Talk about God's favor! As Mary and Joseph chose to do His will and to trust in His ways, God continued to guide them and bless them with signs of His glorious presence. He will do the same for you. Call upon His name. Surrender yourself to His will. Keep Him close to you in your thoughts and in your prayers. He will light up your world.

Let us pray.

> Dear Lord,
> I will call upon Your name,
> and in You,
> I will dwell secure.
> Amen.

29. ACCEPT

*But to those who did accept him he gave power
to become children of God, to those who
believe in his name* (Jn 1:12).

As Catholics, we believe in a triune God — three
persons in one God. While the Trinity remains
a mystery of our Faith, we do know God as the Father,
the Creator; Jesus as the Son, the Redeemer; and the
Holy Spirit as the Power, the Sanctifier.

> After all the people had been baptized
> and Jesus also had been baptized and was
> praying, heaven was opened and the holy
> Spirit descended upon him in bodily form
> like a dove. And a voice came from heaven,
> "You are my beloved Son; with you I am
> well pleased" (Lk 3:21-22).

At His Baptism, Jesus is identified as the Son
of God. God gave Him a human nature and sent
Him here to earth to bring us back to Himself. Jesus
began His public ministry with His own Baptism.
Jesus Himself did not need to be cleansed of sin. He
had no sin. We, however, do. Jesus showed us that
the first step to becoming a child of God is Baptism.
Through our Baptism, we are cleansed of original
sin, and we receive the Holy Spirit. Think about that
— God's Spirit comes to dwell within each one of

us. It is through that indwelling that we are sanctified or changed, and able to grow into the holy people that God created us to be.

In the Gospel of John, we are reminded that there were those who did not accept Jesus. For today, let us think about those who did. It was they who received great reward.

> If you love me, you will keep my commandments. And I will ask the Father, and he will give you another Advocate to be with you always, the Spirit of truth, which the world cannot accept, because it neither sees nor knows it. But you know it, because it remains with you, and will be in you (Jn 14:15-17).

Let us pray.

Dear Jesus,
Please send an outpouring of Your Spirit
to forever remain within me.
Amen.

30. COMMIT

Now Stephen, filled with grace and power,
was working great wonders and signs
among the people (Acts 6:8).

In Acts 6:8-10; 7:54-59, we read about Stephen who was devoted to prayer and to spreading the Good News of salvation through Christ Jesus. He was filled with God's Spirit and did not hesitate to proclaim the truth. In life and in death, his commitment to Christ was evident.

Stephen was brought before the Sanhedrin where he was charged with "blasphemy" against Moses and against God. He attempted to defend his teachings, explaining that God's promise, from Abraham through Jesus, was salvation to all who accepted Him and followed His ways. Stephen pointed out to his persecutors that they, as their ancestors, were in opposition to the Holy Spirit and His work. Their refusal to accept Jesus could be likened to the refusal of their ancestors to accept and follow the Law of Moses. As you can imagine, his persecutors were angered by Stephen's claim.

In that moment, Stephen had a vision. He revealed to the angry crowd what he saw: "Behold, I see the heavens opened and the Son of Man standing at the right hand of God" (Acts 7:56).

In Mark 14, we learn that just before the death of Jesus, Jesus Himself had been brought before the Sanhedrin. He had been asked whether or not He truly was the Messiah. Jesus said, "I am; and you will see the Son of Man seated at the right hand of the Power and coming with the clouds of heaven" (Mk 14:62). Stephen's vision was a complete confirmation that Jesus was the Messiah, and He was, indeed, where He said He would be — at the right hand of the Father. The Sanhedrin refused to listen. Instead, they brought Stephen out of the city and stoned him to death.

Stephen was a true disciple. By the power of the Holy Spirit working within him, he became like Christ. He spoke the truth boldly, surrendered his spirit to the Lord, and asked the Father to forgive his enemies. He faced his death with courage and conviction.

Let us pray.

Dear Lord,
Help me to commit myself to You,
learn from You,
and through Your Spirit,
become more and more like You.
Amen.

31. BELIEVE

Then the other disciple also went in,
the one who had arrived at the tomb first,
and he saw and believed (Jn 20:8).

In John 20:2-8, we read about the "Beloved Disciple," who took one look in the tomb and knew that the body of his Lord had not been stolen, but that Jesus had risen from the dead. The name of the "Beloved Disciple" was John, the son of Zebedee and brother of James. According to Luke's Gospel, John was at the Lake of Gennesaret when Jesus climbed aboard Peter's boat, went just a little way from the shore, and began to preach. Jesus then asked Peter to lower the fishing nets. Given that Peter had already been out for a full day without success, he was reluctant, but complied. When the nets were pulled up, there were so many fish that a second boat was needed to haul in the catch.

John was in the second boat. There he witnessed that miracle, and many more to come. John left everything behind, that very day, to follow Jesus. He spent the next three years watching Jesus and learning from Him. He was present at the Transfiguration where he watched as Jesus' countenance changed. His actual physical features and his clothing became brighter than bright. John listened as Jesus spoke with Moses and Elijah about His own death. John himself heard the voice of God proclaim, "This is my beloved Son, with whom I am well pleased; listen to him" (Mt 17:5).

The more we read of John's Gospel, the clearer it becomes that John did listen to every word that Jesus spoke, including Jesus' explanation of His own suffering and death:

> You heard me tell you, "I am going away and I will come back to you." If you loved me, you would rejoice that I am going to the Father; for the Father is greater than I. And now I have told you this before it happens, so that when it happens you may believe (Jn 14:28-29).

Is it any wonder that when John entered the tomb, he saw and believed?

Let us pray.

Dear Jesus,
Help me to see
and to believe.
Amen.

32. DESIRE

But if we walk in the light as he is in the light,
then we have fellowship with one another,
and the blood of his Son Jesus cleanses
us from all sin (1 Jn 1:7).

Jesus invites us to walk with Him on this journey. When we draw near to Him, He shines His light upon our path, allowing us to clearly see the direction we are meant to take. He offers Himself as the advocate, providing guidance and support as we make our way home to Heaven. In the Gospel of John, we learn of the promises that Jesus makes to those who walk in His light. Take some time today to ponder each of these promises.

> I am the light of the world. Whoever follows me will not walk in darkness, but will have the light of life (Jn 8:12).

> Whoever has my commandments and observes them is the one who loves me. And whoever loves me will be loved by my Father, and I will love him and reveal myself to him (Jn 14:21).

> I will not leave you orphans; I will come to you (Jn 14:18).

Jesus answered and said to him, "Whoever loves me will keep my word, and my Father will love him, and we will come to him and make our dwelling with him" (Jn 14:23).

Ask yourself, do you desire His light, love, and revelation? Do you want Him to come and live in you?

Let us pray.

Lord,
I do desire that which You offer.
Please make Your dwelling within me.
Amen.

33. CHOOSE

This man was righteous and devout,
awaiting the consolation of Israel, and the
holy Spirit was upon him (Lk 2:25).

I love the story of Simeon (Lk 2:22-35). The Holy Spirit had revealed to Simeon that before he was to die, he would indeed see the Messiah. Simeon believed and waited upon the Lord. Then one day, Mary and Joseph brought their first born child to the temple, as was the custom. Simeon saw the Holy Family and knew that the long-awaited Messiah had entered the world!

The Messiah came into the world to save us from our sin and to bring us into the Kingdom of God. Salvation truly begins with Christ Jesus. Take some time today to think about the faithfulness of Mary, Joseph, and Simeon. Then take some time to tell the Lord what you believe about Him, and the role you desire for Him to have in your life. Use the prayer below to guide your conversation.

Let us pray.

Lord Jesus,
I believe that You are the Messiah.
I believe that You are the light of the world.
I am sorry for my sins and ask You to dispel

any and all darkness I have allowed into my life.
I believe that You were sent to this earth with a
message from God the Father.
I believe the message is that God loves me.
I believe that God, Emmanuel, is with me.
I choose to follow You, Lord God, and to seek
only You and Your holy ways.
Send me Your Spirit.
Shine Your light in me.
Teach me Your ways.
Purify me.
Sanctify me.
In Your Holy Name, Jesus, I pray.
Amen.

34. CONQUER

I write to you, young men, because you are strong and the word of God remains in you, and you have conquered the evil one (1 Jn 2:14).

When I was a little girl, I saw a picture of the temptation of Jesus in the children's Bible. The devil in the picture frightened me. I wish that at the time I had a better understanding of the Scripture, for if I did then I wouldn't have allowed the onset of fear. Clearly, Jesus was not afraid of the devil nor could Jesus be tempted with the things of this world. He had only one desire — to do the will of the Father. We will be tempted, just as Jesus was, but we need not focus on the devil nor be afraid. We may think Jesus would have an advantage over us in terms of resisting temptation, given His divinity. However, as baptized children of God, we have that same advantage. Through Baptism we are made new, and we become a "partaker of the divine nature, member of Christ and coheir with him, and temple of the Holy Spirit" (*CCC*, 1265).

The *Catechism of the Catholic Church* further explains:

> The Most Holy Trinity gives the baptized sanctifying grace, the grace of justification: — enabling them to believe in God, to hope in him, and to love him through

the theological virtues; — giving them the power to live and act under the prompting of the Holy Spirit through the gifts of the Holy Spirit; — allowing them to grow in goodness through the moral virtues. Thus the whole organism of the Christian's supernatural life has its roots in Baptism (*CCC*, 1266).

Think about that — through our Baptism and the gifts given to us through the Holy Spirit, we are given power to resist sin and grow in virtue.

Take some time now to think about the words "power" and "virtue" and then read a little more of the Church's teachings about conquering sin: "By his obedience unto death, Christ communicated to his disciples the gift of royal freedom, so that they might 'by the self-abnegation of a holy life, overcome the reign of sin in themselves.'" It is further explained:

That man is rightly called a king who makes his own body an obedient subject, and, by governing himself with suitable rigor, refuses to let his passions breed rebellion in his soul, for he exercises a kind of royal power over himself. And because he knows how to rule his own person as king, so too does he sit as its judge. He will not let himself be imprisoned by sin, or thrown headlong into wickedness (*CCC*, 908).

Let us pray.

Dear God,
Please give me that
which I need to conquer sin
and to allow only You
to reign over my life.
Amen.

35. PERSEVERE

Let the word of Christ dwell in you richly...
(Col 3:16).

During the Mass right before the Gospel is read, we engage in the meaningful gesture of making the Sign of the Cross on our foreheads, on our lips, and on our hearts. I love this action, for in doing this we are asking God for His Word to penetrate our minds, to go forth from our lips, and to dwell in our hearts. When we read or listen with this intent, we find instruction and inspiration.

Spending time in the Scriptures, on Sundays and every day, helps us to connect more deeply to the Lord and to grow in His ways. In the *Catechism of the Catholic Church* we read:

> Human virtues acquired by education, by deliberate acts and by perseverance ever-renewed in repeated efforts are purified and elevated by divine grace. With God's help, they forge character and give facility in the practice of the good. The virtuous man is happy to practice them (*CCC*, 1810).

Let us pray.

Father God,
Teach me Your ways.

Help me to love as You love.
Help me to be compassionate and kind.
Help me to be humble, gentle, and patient.
Help me to seek forgiveness and to freely give it.
Fill my mind with Your wisdom and my heart
with Your peace.
And Lord, may everything I say and do glorify
Your Holy Name.
Thank You, Lord, for Your love, for Your
guidance, and for Your grace.
Amen.

36. ABIDE

*And the Word became flesh and made
his dwelling among us...* (Jn 1:14).

Jesus Himself instituted the Eucharist. Jesus Himself instructed us to eat of His flesh and to drink of His blood. We read these instructions in Matthew 26:26-28, "'Take and eat; this is my body.' Then he took a cup, gave thanks, and gave it to them saying, 'Drink from it, all of you, for this is my blood of the covenant, which will be shed on behalf of many for the forgiveness of sins.'"

During the Liturgy of the Eucharist, gifts of bread and wine are brought to the altar. The priest, acting in the person of Christ, prays the Eucharistic prayer. In this prayer of thanksgiving and consecration, the priest asks God to send the Holy Spirit to change the bread and wine into the Body and the Blood of Christ. When the priest raises the Host, the bells are rung. We are made aware, through faith, that the Holy Spirit has indeed come down upon the gifts; Transubstantiation has occurred. They are no longer ordinary bread and wine but have become the Body and Blood of Christ.

The *Catechism of the Catholic Church* states:

> Holy communion augments our union
> with Christ. The principal fruit of receiving

the Eucharist in Holy Communion is an intimate union with Christ Jesus. Indeed, the Lord said: He who eats my flesh and drinks my blood abides in me and I in him (*CCC*, 1391; Jn 6:56).

It further states:

What material food produces in our bodily life, Holy Communion wonderfully achieves in our spiritual life. Communion with the flesh of the risen Christ ..., preserves, increases, and renews the life of grace received at Baptism. This growth in Christian life needs the nourishment of Eucharistic Communion, the bread for our pilgrimage until the moment of death, when it will be given to us as Viaticum. (*CCC*, 1392; *PO* 5).

As we read these Scriptures and explanations, is it any wonder that based on the Third Commandment we are obligated to go to Mass?

Let us pray.

Dear Lord,
I will eat Your flesh,
and I will abide in You.
Amen.

37. BEHOLD

And Mary kept all these things, reflecting on
them in her heart (Lk 2:19).

When I was a young girl, I used to pray the
Rosary at bedtime, especially when I was
scared. I would tightly hold on to the beads and pray
the "Our Fathers" and the "Hail Marys." Though
I would usually fall asleep before getting too far, my
mother said not to worry — the angels would pick up
where I left off. Looking back, I can imagine those
angels surrounding my bed. I can also imagine Mary
holding on as tightly to me as I was to the beads.

A friend of mine asked me to begin praying the
Rosary for our parish priests. Her goal was to have
three or four different people from our parish praying every day for our priests. She asked me to commit
to Fridays. I initially said "no." First, I thought it
took too long to pray the Rosary. Second, I didn't
want to say I'd do it and then forget. She kept asking.
I finally agreed, and she gave me a pamphlet pub-
lished by Marian Press — *Pray the Rosary Daily.* The
pamphlet had instructions about how to pray the
Rosary. Though I had prayed the Rosary in a simple
way as a child, through this pamphlet, I began to
learn about the Mysteries of the Rosary and the fruit
of each mystery. I was moved as I reflected upon the
lives of Mary, Jesus, and the disciples; it was like I was
discovering a new family history.

Some wonder why as Catholics we focus so much on Mary and why we pray to her. A short, simple answer is this — Mary is Jesus' mother. That makes her our mother too. Jesus does want us to have a relationship with her. Consider that as Mary stood at the foot of the cross, Jesus said to her, "'Woman, behold, your son.' Then he said to the disciple, 'Behold, your mother.' And from that hour the disciple took her into his home" (Jn 19:26-27). I am not a theologian or a Mariologist; however, it just makes sense to me that if Jesus wanted the disciple whom He loved to take His mother into his house, He wants us to do the same.

On another note, I still to this day turn to my earthly mother when I have something going on in my life. My earthly mother listens with an attentive ear, offering comfort, wisdom and prayers. I believe the Blessed Mother wants us to reach out to her in the same way.

Let us pray.

Dear Jesus,
Help me to enter into
the mysteries of the most Holy Rosary
and to know Our Blessed Mother.
Amen.

38. REMAIN

As for you, the anointing that you received
from him remains in you...
(1 Jn 2:27).

When Jesus was baptized in the Jordan River, the Holy Spirit descended upon Him like a dove. Likewise, at your Confirmation, the Holy Spirit descended upon you. As part of your ceremony, the bishop laid his hands on you and anointed you with oil, a ritual serving as a sign of the Spirit. As we grow in our faith, we are often asked to believe without seeing. God demonstrated this point to Abraham, who is known as the Father of our Faith.

God came to Abraham in a vision and promised him great reward. Abraham questioned the value of such reward, as he had no children with which to share it all. Then God brought Abraham outside and said to him, "Look up at the sky and count the stars, if you can. Just so, he added, will your descendants be. Abram put his faith in the Lord, who attributed it to him as an act of righteousness" (Gen 15:5-6).

What I love about this Scripture is that, as we read further into the passage, we learn that this conversation between Abraham and God was held in the daylight. So when God brought Abraham outside, there were no stars to be seen. Though Abraham could not see the stars, he knew they existed.

Though you cannot see the Holy Spirit, rest assured that He is with you. When you make a commitment to follow Jesus Christ, God marks you as His own and sends to you His Holy Spirit, who is with you always!

Let us pray.

Dear God,
Thank You for Your promises,
Your teachings,
and Your Holy Spirit.
Amen.

39. SEEK

I did not know him, but the one who sent me to baptize with water told me, 'On whomever you see the Spirit come down and remain, he is the one who will baptize with the holy Spirit.' Now I have seen and testified that he is the Son of God (Jn 1:33-34).

We are born of the flesh. Through Baptism, we become children of God. Nicodemus, a ruler of the Jews, came to Jesus seeking to understand. Nicodemus believed that Jesus was a teacher. He believed that Jesus had to have come from God in order to perform such wondrous works. What he did not understand was what it meant "to be born again". In John 3:3, Jesus explained to Nicodemus, "… no one can see the kingdom of God without being born from above."

When we are baptized, the Holy Spirit comes down upon us. As we open ourselves up to the Spirit and immerse ourselves in the Scriptures, we begin to understand what it means to belong to the Kingdom of God. We begin to understand who Christ is, and what discipleship looks like. In John 14:26, we learn that the Holy Spirit is our guide, our Advocate: "The Advocate, the holy Spirit that the Father will send in my name — he will teach you everything and remind you of all that [I] told you."

That which Jesus told His disciples is written in the Scriptures.

> Remain in me, as I remain in you. Just as a branch cannot bear fruit on its own unless it remains on the vine, so neither can you unless you remain in me. I am the vine, you are the branches. Whoever remains in me and I in him will bear much fruit, because without me you can do nothing. Anyone who does not remain in me will be thrown out like a branch and wither; people will gather them and throw them into a fire and they will be burned. As the Father loves me, so I also love you. Remain in my love (Jn 15:4-6,9).

Let us pray.

Dear Lord,
I will seek Your ways,
let Your spirit guide me
as I continue to grow in my faith.
Amen.

40. TASTE

*He first found his own brother Simon
and told him, "We have found the Messiah"*
(Jn 1:41).

In John 1:35-42, we read about Andrew, who followed Jesus because John the Baptist proclaimed that Jesus was the Messiah. Andrew went to see for himself and came to that same conclusion. Andrew's brother, Simon, soon followed suit. As we proclaim that same truth, we are marked as Christ's own. As God's Spirit stirs within us, our world changes. No longer are we residents of the physical world, but of the spiritual one. What transpires in this world goes beyond anything that our own abilities could bring us to understand.

I remember a friend once shared with me that she thought it was difficult to put into words what it was like, living life with Jesus. She likened it to describing different flavors of ice cream to someone who had never had it before. Her conclusion was that there are some things you just have to taste for yourself.

We are invited to taste and see how good the Lord truly is. We do that by opening our hearts to Him and asking Him to come into our everyday lives.

Let us pray.

Dear Jesus,
Please stay close to me throughout each day,
that I may continue to taste Your goodness.
Amen.

41. LOVE

Children, let us love not in word or speech
but in deed and truth (1 Jn 3:18).

When we become God's children, He reveals His ways to us. Through daily Scripture readings and through prayer, His values, characteristics, and examples of love become clear to us. When we allow God to love us, we cannot help but to love Him in return. We become His disciples because we want to love like He does. We become willing to learn from Him. He teaches us through our daily experiences with Him, through the world around us, and through the Scriptures. Sometimes, though, our greatest lessons are learned through our mistakes.

When I first came to know the Lord, I tried to convince a family member that he too should follow Jesus. I was highly judgmental. I felt he needed Jesus, and I wanted so much for him to discover and share in what I was experiencing. My intentions were good, but my approach was not.

If I could go back, I would have not judged. Instead, I would have just witnessed what had happened to me, told my story, and then asked God to help me love as deeply as I possibly could. In retrospect, I see that those who drew me to Christ caught my attention because of their witness and their love.

Jesus tells us that we should love one another. Sometimes that is hard to do. At times, people hurt us, disappoint us, or simply don't do what we want them to do. But when we try to look at people through God's eyes, we do see a different picture. God's picture is painted with love, understanding, kindness, and compassion. Through God's grace, we can carry out His commandment to love and love deeply. It is His love that will draw others near.

Let us pray.

Lord God,
I need Your grace
to love as You do.
Amen.

42. DISCOVER

They opened their treasures and offered him gifts of gold, frankincense, and myrrh (Mt 2:11).

In Matthew 2:9-12, we read of the Epiphany, the event wherein the three Magi were led by the star to where they found the Savior. They bowed down before His majesty and presented Him with fine gifts. I remember my own finding of the Savior. I did not have fine gifts to give to Him, but I gave Him what I had: first my heart, then my hands, then my whole self. Not long after, I read Ephesians 3:14-19, and knew at once this was a message to be shared.

> For this reason I kneel before the Father, from whom every family in heaven and on earth is named, that he may grant you in accord with the riches of his glory to be strengthened with power through his Spirit in the inner self, and that Christ may dwell in your hearts through faith; that you, rooted and grounded in love, may have strength to comprehend with all the holy ones what is the breadth and length and height and depth, and to know the love of Christ that surpasses knowledge, so that you may be filled with all the fullness of God (Eph 3:14-19).

This Scripture is full of God's hopes for you. He wants you to be strong on the inside. He wants you to believe you were made out of His love and that you are His precious creation. He wants you to welcome Him into your heart where He so desires to dwell. He wants to be your foundation, the solid rock you cling to through the good and the bad. He wants you to discover the depth of His love for you and be filled with all that He is and all that He has for you.

Let us conclude our reflections with the Gospel of Matthew, as it is a perfect springboard into the question of where to go from here. As you read the account of Jesus' Ascension into Heaven, picture yourself being there, seeing the risen Christ and listening to His words. As you enter into this story, remember — you are His disciple. These words are meant for you:

> The eleven disciples went to Galilee, to the mountain to which Jesus had ordered them. When they saw him, they worshiped, but they doubted. Then Jesus approached and said to them, "All power in heaven and on earth has been given to me. Go, therefore, and make disciples of all nations, baptizing them in the name of the Father, and of the Son, and of the holy Spirit, teaching them to observe all that I have commanded you. And behold, I am

with you always, until the end of the age"
(Mt 28:16-20).

Let us pray.

Lord God,
May I continue to discover You
each and every day
and to help others do the same!
Amen.

PART THREE
Essentials for Discipleship

My Story — Continued.

I had once, long ago, thought the difference between Catholics and non-Catholics was that as Catholics, we focused on God the Father, who I thought was more distant, who perhaps heard our prayers from afar. I thought non-Catholics were more about Jesus, with whom they seemed to have a closer, more open and intimate relationship. Oh my, how wrong had I been? Once I began to understand who Jesus was and the role He played in my salvation (and that of the whole world, of course), I jumped into a deeper walk with Him, choosing to put Him at the center of my life.

While clearly the Trinity still remains a mystery, the Lord had enlightened me: God is not distant. He is alive in and around us. I knew there were so many other people out in the world who were just like me — people who grew up in the Catholic Church and had yet to discover the treasures of our Faith, including Salvation through Jesus Christ and the promised gift of the Holy Spirit. I remember sitting in the Adoration Chapel at my church, staring at Jesus, present in the Eucharist, and having a conversation with Him about all of this. I had such a strong desire in my heart to tell the whole world what I had come to know. And I expressed that desire to the Lord. I was graced right there in the Chapel that day as I read Ephesians 3:14-19. I knew at once this was to be my mission statement.

> For this reason I kneel before the Father, from whom every family in heaven and on earth is named, that he may grant you in accord with the riches of his glory to be strengthened with power through his Spirit in the inner self, and that Christ may dwell in your hearts through faith; that you, rooted and grounded in love, may have strength to comprehend with all the holy ones what is the breadth and length and height and depth, and to know the love of Christ that surpasses knowledge, so that you may be filled with all the fullness of God (Eph 3:14-19).

Almost twenty years have passed, from the day I sat in the Chapel and read this life-giving passage in Ephesians to the day I write to you this continuation of my story: "Essentials For Discipleship." I thank the Lord for walking so closely with me for all of these years. I thank the Lord for all He has taught me and all He will continue to teach me. I thank Him for His love, His presence, His guidance, and His power to transform me — to help me to become more like Him. I thank the Lord for continuously revealing Himself to me, and teaching me how to live more freely in Him, and how to love more selflessly as He does. I thank the Lord for my unwavering conviction of who He is and who I am because of Him.

I thank you, too, for having journeyed with me for the past 42 days. I hope you have been able to connect with Him in a newer, deeper way. Such is the beauty of our walk with Him; He is always taking us into deeper waters. And when we can give Him our fears in exchange for trust, miracles happen — big and small.

> Then he made the disciples get into the boat and precede him to the other side, while he dismissed the crowds. After doing so, he went up on the mountain by himself to pray. When it was evening he was there alone. Meanwhile the boat, already a few miles offshore, was being tossed about by the waves, for the wind was against it. During the fourth watch of the night, he came toward them, walking on the sea. When the disciples saw him walking on the sea they were terrified. "It is a ghost," they said, and they cried out in fear. At once [Jesus] spoke to them, "Take courage, it

is I; do not be afraid." Peter said to him in reply, "Lord, if it is you, command me to come to you on the water." He said, "Come." Peter got out of the boat and began to walk on the water toward Jesus. But when he saw how [strong] the wind was he became frightened; and, beginning to sink, he cried out, "Lord, save me!" Immediately Jesus stretched out his hand and caught him, and said to him, "O you of little faith, why did you doubt?" After they got into the boat, the wind died down. Those who were in the boat did him homage, saying, "Truly, you are the Son of God" (Mt 14:22-33).

So, how do you get to a point where you will even get into the boat, never mind get out and walk on the water toward Jesus? I will share some things with you, that by the grace of God I have come to know, and I pray you will trust in my witness until these convictions become your own.

#1 Believe That God Loves YOU.

Believe that the Lord loves you, beyond anything that words can describe. Think about it: God experienced His creation pulling away from Him, so He devised a plan to bring it back — "it" meaning you and me. He sent His Son, His child, into this world to tell us that we too are His children and that we were created by Him in His image.

We read in Genesis 1:26-27:

Then God said: "Let us make human beings in our image, after our likeness. Let them have dominion over the fish of the sea, the birds of the air, the tame animals, all the wild animals, and all the creatures that crawl on the earth."
God created man in his image;
In the image of God he created them;
Male and female he created them.

We read further in Genesis 1:31, "God looked at everything he had made, and found it very good." God wants you to know you are part of His story. Among His glorious creation, He created you. And you are good.

You formed my inmost being; you knit me in my mother's womb. I praise you, because I am wonderfully made; wonderful are your works! My very self you know (Ps 139:13-14).

God wants you to know who you are in Him. In 1 John 3:1 we read, "See what love the Father has bestowed on us that we may be called the children of God. Yet so we are … " From Him is where our identity comes, and in Him is where we find our strength.

#2 Live in Union with Him.

> When you call me, and come and pray to
> me, I will listen to you. When you look for
> me, you will find me. Yes, when you seek
> me with all your heart, I will let you find
> me — oracle of the LORD — and I will
> change your lot... (Jer 29:12-14).

Christ lives within you. Yes, He is in and with
you, 24/7. You can talk with Him any time about
anything; He is right there. He will never hide from
you, and He will never tire of you. In fact, before He
left this earth, He assured His disciples of this very
truth. He said, "And behold, I am with you always,
until the end of the age" (Mt 28:20).

We are also assured of this as we read Philippians
4:4-7:

> Rejoice in the Lord always. I shall say again:
> rejoice! Your kindness should be known to
> all. The Lord is near. Have no anxiety at all,
> but in everything, by prayer and petition,
> with thanksgiving, make your requests
> known to God. Then the peace of God
> that surpasses all understanding will guard
> your hearts and minds in Christ Jesus.

This too may take a little while for you to fully
believe. As with any relationship, trust is built over
time. I promise you, the more you approach Him

and invite Him into your everyday life, the more you will recognize His presence, His promptings, and His guidance. "And I will ask the Father, and he will give you another Advocate to be with you always, the Spirit of truth, which the world cannot accept, because it neither sees nor knows it. But you know it, because it remains with you, and will be in you. I will not leave you orphans; I will come to you" (Jn 14:16-18).

#3 Trust In Him.

> But you, Israel, my servant,
> Jacob, whom I have chosen,
> offspring of Abraham my friend —
> You whom I have taken from the ends
> of the earth
> and summoned from its far-off places,
> To whom I have said, You are my servant;
> I chose you, I have not rejected you —
> Do not fear: I am with you;
> Do not be anxious; I am your God.
> I will strengthen you, I will help you,
> I will uphold you with my victorious right
> hand (Is 41:8-10).

Think about this truth — God sent His Son to bring you to Himself. And yes, He has countless other children, but His family is not complete without you. You are so precious to Him. I'll say again, truly, in Him we find our identity and our strength. This is what I cling to first and foremost any time doubt, confusion, or negative thoughts try to set in. Sometimes I do wrestle a little longer than I should, but I always come back to this simple truth: I am a child of God. He loves me, He created me, and He thinks I am good. He chose me, and He will guide me in all things. This may be hard for you to believe at first, especially if you have gone through life without affirmations or if you have experienced trauma and abuse. Know that God loves you so much and will heal your deepest wounds.

> Heal me, LORD, that I may be healed;
> save me that I may be saved,
> for you are my praise (Jer 17:14).

It may take you some time to put your trust in the Lord, but know this — through His Holy Spirit living in you, you will be made strong:

> It is not that I have already taken hold of it or have already attained perfect maturity, but I continue my pursuit in hope that I may possess it, since I have indeed been taken possession of by Christ [Jesus]. Brothers, I for my part do not consider myself to have taken possession. Just one thing: forgetting what lies behind but straining forward to what lies ahead, I continue my pursuit toward the goal, the prize of God's upward calling, in Christ Jesus (Phil 3:12-14).

PART FOUR

The Role of the Blessed Mother — Including Prayers for Continued Conversion

Mary plays many roles — one of which is great warrior and protector. Undoubtedly, we need her. "A thief comes only to steal and slaughter and destroy; I came so that they might have life and have it more abundantly" (Jn 10:10).

Remember the story of Adam and Eve in the Garden (Gen 3:1-24). Adam and Eve were tempted to doubt God, His Word and His plan for them. We will be tempted in that same way by the evil one, who I hate to talk about or give any attention to whatsoever. All you need to know about him is that he is a liar and a thief. He does not want you to believe what God tells you. And he wants to steal your joy and your strength and everything else that goes along with being a child of God. Here is where the Blessed Mother comes in. See, she is a momma bear, and we are her cubs. You do NOT need to be afraid. You do NOT need to even engage in any type of conversation with the evil one. When I feel afraid or threatened in any way, I immediately run to Mary. She knows I am just a baby; a little "fraidy cat." She surrounds me with her motherly love and covers me with her fierce protection. I keep my eyes on the Lord, and she takes care of everything else. She has never failed me, and she will not fail you either. In fact, sometimes I will just close my eyes and reach out for the hands of Jesus and Mary. I feel them each take a hand, and with me in the middle, we walk on this long road. I cannot see the end, only its light in the far off distance. I feel peaceful and secure. How awesome it is for us all to know that we are not alone.

I would be remiss if I did not share with you the extent to which praying the Rosary has aided in my faith formation. As part of my regular routine, I pray the Rosary for the conversion of all hearts. When I first began to pray this devotion, I never imagined how much it would impact my own ongoing conversion. Throughout the years, as I prayed the Rosary, my reflections on each of the mysteries have turned into prayers. These, I share with you. As you read them, know that these prayers in no way replace the Rosary, for I cling to each bead and pray each prayer with all my heart. These are the prayers that flow forth from my heart after reflecting upon each mystery.

Prayers from the Heart — Born Out of Reflections on the Joyful Mysteries.

THE FIRST JOYFUL MYSTERY:
The Annunciation

Father God,
Please help me to be open to Your plan for my life, today and every day. Help me to surrender to You in all things, big and small.
Amen.

THE SECOND JOYFUL MYSTERY:
The Visitation

Father God,
When I have a lot going on, help me to trust that You and Your mother will take care of all of my needs, so that I may be Your hands and feet. Help me to be attentive, assistive, and encouraging to all those You have placed in my path.
Amen.

THE THIRD JOYFUL MYSTERY:
The Birth of Jesus

Father God,
Help me to be humble and to trust in Your plan, even when it is hard to see it clearly. Rather than worry about the unknown or about circumstances that are beyond my control, help me to rejoice in You, knowing that Your hand is upon me.
Amen.

THE FOURTH JOYFUL MYSTERY:
The Presentation

Father God,
Today and every day, I offer to You my husband, my children, their spouses and their children. I offer to You my parents, my siblings and their families, my friends and their families, my co-workers and their families, my community members, and all of Your children — from the North to the South to the East to the West, please keep them safe and bring them all home to You.
Amen.

THE FIFTH JOYFUL MYSTERY:
Finding the Child Jesus in the Temple

Father God,
Fill me with Your wisdom today and every day. And please let everyone in this whole world find You, embrace You, and love You.
Amen.

Simple Prayers from the Heart — Born out of Reflections on the Sorrowful Mysteries.

THE FIRST SORROWFUL MYSTERY:
The Agony in the Garden

Jesus,

I am so sorry for my sins and for those of everyone in this world. May I never forget the agony which You endured to atone for my sins. Help me on this day and every day to turn from temptation and sin and to follow You.

Amen.

THE SECOND SORROWFUL MYSTERY:
The Scourging at the Pillar

Jesus,

I am mortified by the thought of Your body, beaten and scourged. I love You, my Lord. Help me to live my life continuing on in Your mission. Please give me strength today and every day to stand against hatred and injustice, and may everything I do bring forth Your love and goodness into this world.

Amen.

THE THIRD SORROWFUL MYSTERY:
The Crowning with Thorns

Jesus,

I am saddened by the actions of the soldiers who were mocking You. Please know that You truly

are my king; it is for You that I will live this day.
Amen.

THE FOURTH SORROWFUL MYSTERY:
Carrying of the Cross

Jesus,

I am heartbroken as I think of You, carrying the
weight of the cross and falling to the ground
three times. When I fall, please give me strength
to rise up and continue on in Your Name. And,
Jesus, please give me strength and courage to
help others in need.
Amen.

THE FIFTH SORROWFUL MYSTERY:
The Crucifixion

Jesus

Thank You for sacrificing Your life for me, so
that I can live with You today and every day,
throughout all of eternity. Please help me to
remember Your sacrifice, and to make sacrifices,
big and small, that are pleasing to You and that
will help to build Your Kingdom.
Amen.

Simple Prayers from the Heart — Born out of Reflections on the Glorious Mysteries.

THE FIRST GLORIOUS MYSTERY:
The Resurrection

Jesus,
Thank You for conquering death and for showing me that, with You, I will not be held down. Help me to glorify Your holy name as I live this hope-filled truth.
Amen.

THE SECOND GLORIOUS MYSTERY:
The Ascension

Jesus,
I love thinking of You taking Your place at the right hand of the Father. Thank You for inviting me into Your heavenly court. May I live this day in honor of Your love and generosity.
Amen.

THE THIRD GLORIOUS MYSTERY:
The Descent of the Holy Spirit

Jesus,
Thank You for the gift of Your Holy Spirit. Fill me with Your spirit each and every moment of this day. Guide me and lead me in Your ways; may I live Your message and share it as I do Your work today.
Amen.

THE FOURTH GLORIOUS MYSTERY:
The Assumption

Father God,
Thank You for the gift of Mary. Please help me to live as Mary did, devoted to You and living in a way most pleasing to You. Please let Mary remain at my side, loving and guiding me, and leading me closer to You.
Amen.

THE FIFTH GLORIOUS MYSTERY:
The Coronation

Mary,
Thank you for your extraordinary example of discipleship. Thank you for always accepting the will of the Father and, with grace, carrying out the work He has prepared for you. Thank you for your love, instruction, and protection. Thank you for continuously taking my prayers to the Father.
I love you.

Simple Prayers from the Heart — Born out of Reflections on the Luminous Mysteries.

THE FIRST LUMINOUS MYSTERY:
The Baptism of Jesus

> Father God,
> Thank You for sending Your Son to show us all the way to You. Thank You for sending Your Spirit to dwell within me. Through Your Spirit, may I act in accordance with Your will today and every day.
> Amen.

THE SECOND LUMINOUS MYSTERY:
The Wedding at Cana

> Father God,
> Thank You for sending Your Son to give witness to Your love and Your transforming power. Today, to You I bring all of my needs and the needs of all those around me. May I do what You say and give glory to You as I see Your will be done.
> Amen.

THE THIRD LUMINOUS MYSTERY:
Proclaiming the Kingdom

> Father God,
> Thank You for bringing me into Your Kingdom, and for all those who walk with You and work to build Your Kingdom. I lift up to You all of Your servants — the Pope, all bishops, all priests, all

religious brothers and sisters, and all lay people who proclaim Your Word. Please send Your Spirit upon us that we may have all we need today to carry forth Your Word to the world. Amen.

THE FOURTH LUMINOUS MYSTERY:
The Transfiguration

Father God,
Thank you for revealing Yourself to me when I am on the top of the mountain and when I am in the valley. Wherever I am, I will cling to You, and I will glorify Your Holy Name.
Amen.

THE FIFTH LUMINOUS MYSTERY:
Institution of the Eucharist

Jesus,
Thank You for the gift of Holy Communion, where you pour Yourself into me — Body, Blood, Soul, and Divinity. I am thankful and still completely in awe of Your desire for me. Please, Jesus, draw all of humankind to Yourself that all may know this union with You.
Amen.

PART FIVE
One Final Thought

When I was a little girl, I loved to eat BLT's. Decades later, as I sat in the Adoration Chapel and the delightful memory of eating BLT's surfaced, this simple joy of childhood morphed into a great acronym for discipleship. Here it is:

B — Believe that the Lord loves you.
L — Live in union with the Lord.
T — Trust in Him.

One Final Request:

Throughout these 42 days, I have shared with you my love for the Lord and my experiences as I walk with Him. In sharing our stories, we glorify God and through His Spirit, we help others to grow in faith. Please consider sharing your story with me, in part or whole. (maureenfleming333@gmail.com) In confidence, I will read it and will join with you in giving thanks and praise for all that the Lord has done.

To continue with me on this faith journey, please SUBSCRIBE to my YouTube channel: *Jesus Time With Maureen*. (Subscriptions are free. By subscribing you will be given easy access to new Jesus Time with Maureen videos.)

May God's blessings be upon you today and always,
Maureen

References

Bergant, D. (1992). *The Collegeville Bible Commentary: Old Testament*. Order of Saint Benedict, Liturgical Press, Collegeville, Minnesota.

Catechism of the Catholic Church, second edition. Twenty-First printing 2010, Libreria Editrice Vaticana, Citta del Vaticano.

Pamphlet: Divine Mercy Novena and Chaplet, Marian Press. Stockbridge, MA. 1993 Marian Fathers of the Immaculate Conception of the B.V.M.

Durken, D. (2009). *New Collegeville Bible Commentary: New Testament*. Order of Saint Benedict, Liturgical Press, Collegeville, Minnesota.

Hahn, S. (2009). *Catholic Bible Dictionary*. New York: Doubleday.

Marian Press. (2016). *Divine Mercy In My Soul: Diary of the Saint Maria Faustina Kowalska*. Marian Press: Stockbridge, MA.

Pamphlet: Pray the Rosary Daily. Marian Press, Stockbridge, MA, 2006 Marian Fathers of the Immaculate Conception of the B.V.M.

The New American Bible Revised Edition: USCCB: http://www.usccb.org/bible/books-of-the-bible/index.cfm

Join the
Association of Marian Helpers,
headquartered at the
National Shrine of The Divine Mercy,
and share in special blessings!

An invitation from
Fr. Joseph, MIC, director

Marian Helpers is an Association of Christian faithful of the Congregation of Marian Fathers of the Immaculate Conception. By becoming a member, you share in the spiritual benefits of the daily Masses, prayers, and good works of the Marian priests and brothers.

This is a special offer of grace given to you by the Church through the Marian Fathers. Please consider this opportunity to share in these blessings, along with others whom you would wish to join into this spiritual communion.

1-800-462-7426 • marian.org/join